Men-at-Arms • 466

Armies of the Balkan Wars 1912–13

The priming charge for the Great War

Philip S. Jowett • Illustrated by Stephen Walsh

Series editor Martin Windrow·

First published in Great Britain in 2011 by Osprey Publishing,
PO Box 883, Oxford, OX1 9PL, UK
1385 Broadway, 5th Floor, New York, NY 10018, USA
Email: info@ospreypublishing.com

OSPREY is a trademark of Osprey Publishing, a division of
Bloomsbury Publishing Plc

Transferred to digital print on demand 2018

First published 2011
3rd impression 2012

Printed and bound in Great Britain

A CIP catalogue record for this book is available from the
British Library

ISBN: 978 1 84908 418 5
eBook PDF ISBN: 9 781 84908 419 2

Editor: Martin Windrow
Page layout by The Black Spot
Index by David Worthington
Typeset in Helvetica Neue and ITC New Baskerville
Originated by United Graphics Pte

Acknowledgements
This book would not have been possible without the kind
assistance of the following: Adrian Bejenaru, Mark Conrad,
Konstantinos Kokotos, George Loukas, David Nicolle, Nikos
Panos, Darko Pavlovic, Duncan Rogers, Nigel Thomas, Count
Ernesto Vitetti, and Paul.V. Walsh.

Several of the Greek photographs are reproduced by kind
permission of Kedros Publishing from their book Balkan Wars
1912–1913 (ISBN 978-960-04-1683-1). The originals of the
two Ablibris photographs featured on pages 36 and 46 are
available to buy at: ablibris eBay store.

Artist's note
Readers may care to note that the original paintings from
which the colour plates in this book were prepared are
available for private sale. All reproduction copyright
whatsoever is retained by the Publishers. All enquiries
should be addressed to:

www.stephenwalshillustrations.co.uk

The Publishers regret that they can enter into no
correspondence upon this matter.

The Woodland Trust
Osprey Publishing supports the Woodland Trust, the UK's
leading woodland conservation charity. Between 2014 and
2018 our donations are being spent on their Centenary
Woods project in the UK.

www.ospreypublishing.com
To find out more about our authors and books visit our
website. Here you will find extracts, author interviews, details
of forthcoming events and the option to sign-up for our
newsletter.

ARMIES OF THE BALKAN WARS 1912–13

INTRODUCTION

The two Balkan Wars fought in 1912–13 are often described by historians as the prelude to World War I. In fact, some would maintain that they were actually the opening salvo of the conflict that was to engulf the Great Powers in August 1914, since the spark that ignited the Great War was struck in the Balkans, amid the tinder laid by Serbia's success in 1912–13.

In 1912 the Balkan region was divided between the sovereign states of Greece, Serbia, Bulgaria, Romania and Montenegro, and the provinces of the Ottoman Turkish Empire in Europe. The gradual liberation of the Balkan nations from Turkish rule during the 19th century had already cost the Ottoman Empire many of its possessions in Europe, but in 1912 there was still a large tract of territory that was ruled directly from Constantinople (Istanbul). The Ottoman provinces in Europe were inhabited by a mixture of Greeks, Bulgarians, Serbs, Albanians and others, some of them dispersed in an ethnic-religious jigsaw puzzle of scattered communities. Many of the non-Turkish peoples of these lands wanted to be joined with what they regarded as their mother countries, but a sizeable proportion of the population were Muslims, and were content to remain subjects of the Ottoman Empire.

The Balkan sovereign nations had been planning for war against the Ottoman Empire for many years, and had built up their military establishments accordingly. In September 1911 these plans were given new impetus by the Ottoman Army's involvement in a war in North Africa and the Dodecanese islands sparked by the Italian invasion of Turkey's Libyan possessions. Although the campaign in Libya was not given high priority by the Turks, it still tied down troops and some of their best officers. This distraction gave the leaders of the Balkan nations an incentive to begin hostilities before the Italo-Turkish War could be resolved.

In simple terms, the First Balkan War (October 1912–May 1913) was a struggle between the armies of the Balkan League – Greece, Serbia, Bulgaria and Montenegro – and the Ottoman armies in Europe. The aims of the Balkan League were to 'liberate' (or perhaps more accurately, to carve up) Ottoman-ruled provinces in the Balkans, adding

Two volunteers of the Bulgarian *Opolcenie* militia prepare to move off with their comrades in 1912. The man on the left wears a rather extravagant fur busby, which he has decorated with some of the flowers thrown by the enthusiastic crowd. His comrade wears a more conventional fleece hat with a metal badge, and in the background can be seen others wearing flat caps and trilbys. These militiamen in their forties had to campaign in their own clothing, supplemented with whatever equipment the Bulgarian Army stores could spare.

them to their own national territories. This war ended with the military defeat of the Ottoman armies; but the peace was short-lived, as the former allies soon fell out amongst themselves. The Second Balkan War (June–July 1913) was the result of Bulgaria's resentment at its perceived lack of gains from the peace treaty that ended the first conflict. Bulgaria attacked the armies of its former allies Greece and Serbia, but, although initially successful, was very soon forced into retreat. In the meantime, Romania, a powerful nation that had stayed neutral in the First Balkan War, took full advantage of Bulgaria's distraction to capture territory it had long claimed as its own. To add insult to injury for the Bulgarians, the recently defeated Ottoman Empire also took this opportunity to regain Eastern Thrace and the fortress of Adrianople.

CHRONOLOGY

FIRST BALKAN WAR, 1912–13

(In order to simplify the confusing military situation during the First Balkan War, operations are divided here into the *Western Theatre* = Macedonia and Albania, and the *Eastern Theatre* = Thrace.)

1912

13 March Bulgaria and Serbia agree a secret treaty to divide Ottoman-ruled Macedonia up between them, with the fate of a third zone to be decided by agreement with the Russian government.

May Bulgaria and Greece sign a treaty of alliance. With further agreements between Montenegro and the other three nations, the 'Balkan League' is forged.

September Ottoman armies in Europe mobilized (**24th**); Bulgarian Army mobilized (**25th**); Greek Army mobilized (**30th**).

8 October, *Western Theatre* Montenegro declares war on the Ottoman Empire, and its troops invade northern Albania.

8 October 1912–23 April 1913, *Western Theatre* Siege of Scutari; having overrun northern Albania, the Montenegrins lay siege to this Ottoman fortress.

16 October, *Western Theatre* Serbian forces invade Kosovo. (**18 October** Treaty of Lausanne ends the Italo-Turkish War, largely in Italy's favour.)

18 October, *Eastern Theatre* Bulgaria declares war on the Ottoman Empire, and three Bulgarian armies cross the border into Ottoman-controlled Thrace. The Bulgarian Second Army surrounds the fortress city of Adrianople, held by a 50,000-strong Ottoman garrison.

18 October, *Western Theatre* The Greek Army crosses the frontier and defeats Ottoman forces. The Bulgarian First and Third Armies, 90,000 strong, advance on a 36-mile front against the main Ottoman army in Eastern Thrace. The Ottoman defeat at the decisive battle of **Kirkilisse** and subsequent withdrawal leave the besieged fortress of Adrianople isolated, and only the Chataldzha defensive lines, *c.*19 miles from Constantinople, stand between the Bulgarians and the Ottoman capital.

23 October, *Western Theatre* Ottoman troops retreat in face of advancing Greeks, north to Monastir.

23–24 October, *Western Theatre* Decisive battle for Macedonia fought at **Kumanovo**, between the 130,000-strong Serbian First Army, and the Ottoman Army of the Vardar with half that number (but both armies are equal in artillery and machine guns). The Ottomans attack, but fail to take the Serbs by surprise. The defeated Ottomans withdraw into southern Macedonia, losing 12,000 dead and wounded and 98 field guns.

24 October, *Western Theatre* Montenegrin and Serbian forces join up at Plevje, and the remaining Ottoman troops cross over into Austro-Hungarian territory to be interned.

29 October–2 November, *Eastern Theatre* In Thrace, the battle of **Lyule Burgas (Buni Hisar)** is the largest military encounter in Europe since the Franco-Prussian War, involving some 130,000 Ottoman troops and about 110,000 Bulgarians. After heavy fighting the Turks fall back, suffering 22,000 casualties; the victorious Bulgarians lose 20,162, including 2,534 dead.

3 November, *Eastern Theatre* In Thrace, the Ottoman East Army withdraws behind the Chataldzha defensive lines on the approaches to Constantinople.

9 November, *Western Theatre* In Macedonia, the Greek 7th Division marches into the city of Salonika, taking 27,000 Ottoman prisoners. A few hours later their Bulgarian allies arrive, causing the first tensions between the two armies.

16–19 November, *Western Theatre* In Macedonia, the Serbian First Army of 108,000 men defeats the 39,000 remnants of the Ottomans' Vardar

It is too simplistic to regard the Balkan Wars as 'struggles of Christian liberation from the Turkish yoke'. Many inhabitants of the Ottoman provinces in Europe were Muslims, and some Christian communities were unwilling to come under the rule of nations following one of the other traditions of the Orthodox religion. This commander of volunteers from Salonika poses wearing a well-tailored khaki woollen uniform with a red fez. Muslim volunteers often wore the star-and-crescent symbol – in this case, in brass on the cartridge box and its sling. For an irregular he is well armed, with a Turkish Mauser M1890 rifle and two bandoliers of five-round clips.

Army at the battle of **Bitola.** The Ottomans suffer 3,000 killed and wounded, and the Serbs take 5,600 prisoners, while 5,000 of the Turkish *rediff* troops desert. This Serbian victory effectively ends any hope of further Ottoman resistance in Macedonia.

November, *Western Theatre* The Serbians send three divisions totalling 30,000 men to reinforce the Montenegrins besieging Scutari, where the Ottoman garrison has increased to 29,000 men including 5,000 Albanian volunteers – only slightly fewer than the besieging Montenegrins.

17–18 November, *Eastern Theatre* Prematurely attacking the 90,000 Ottoman troops defending the Chataldzha lines, the Bulgarians suffer heavy casualties.

4 December Ceasefire agreed between the Ottoman Empire and the Balkan League, apart from Greece.

17 December 1912–13 January 1913 Two separate London peace conferences are held concurrently, one attended by the major powers and the other by the Balkan states.

The Ottoman delegates at first resist the latters' demands, but eventually agree to the loss of Adrianople.

1913

23 January The nationalist faction known as the 'Young Turks' seize control of the government in Constantinople, and immediately reject the peace terms. The London conference breaks up.

3 February Hostilities recommence.

6 March, *Western Theatre* Greek forces capture the important Ottoman fortress of Janina in Epirus, taking 30,000 Turkish prisoners and 200 guns. This victory allows the Greeks to transfer most of their army to Macedonia.

11 March, *Eastern Theatre* Bulgarian forces begin assault on Adrianople.

15–21 March, *Western Theatre* The Greeks take several towns in southern Albania, completing their conquest of disputed 'Northern Epirus'.

26 March, *Eastern Theatre* With the assistance of Serbian units, the Bulgarians take Adrianople after heavy fighting; they lose 9,500 troops, and capture 60,000 Turks.

10 April, *Western Theatre* Because the European powers have agreed to award Scutari to an 'independent' Albania, their navies blockade the Montenegrin-Albanian coast to pressure Montenegro into ending the siege of the city.

14 May, *Western Theatre* Montenegrin troops reluctantly evacuate lines around Scutari, and the European powers establish international control in the city.

30 May Signing of Treaty of London ends the First Balkan War. Under its terms, the Ottoman Turks lose their European territory west of the Enos-Midia line, as well as the island of Crete (they have already lost Rhodes and the Dodecanese to Italy). Albania is given independence, but under the control of the five Great Powers. The casualties in the First Balkan War have been heavy: the Ottoman Empire has lost 50,000 killed and 100,000 wounded, as well as 115,000 of its troops captured. Greece has lost 2,360 dead and 23,502 wounded, Bulgaria 14,000 dead and 50,000 wounded, and Serbia some 5,000 dead and 18,000 wounded.

This group, captioned 'The Scout Unit of Artillery Captain Constantine Mazarkis', shows a wide variety of uniforms in service with the Greek Army. Most of the men are wearing the M1908 khaki uniform with képi-style caps, but some (e.g. right foreground) wear the distinctive *farizan* fez and *doulama* tunic of the Evzones. Other uniforms include the obsolete M1868 summer whites worn by the officer under the tree, and the M1897 dark blue winter uniform worn by the sergeant in the left foreground.

Photographed here with an Evzone NCO, this young Greek boy soldier wearing a sun-flapped M1910 cap is Gerasimos Raphtopoulos, who was promoted and awarded a Mannlicher rifle for several acts of bravery. Raphtopoulos was aged only 12 when he volunteered to join the Greek Army and was accepted into the 18th Infantry Regiment. It was reported that after being captured during the Second Balkan War he escaped, killing the three Bulgarian soldiers guarding him. On 28 August 1913 he was promoted to the rank of corporal, making him the youngest NCO in Greek military history.

Montenegro's losses have been particularly high in proportion to its small population: of an army of only 40,000 men, it has lost 2,836 dead with 6,602 wounded – 22 per cent of the army, and nearly 4 per cent of the entire population.

SECOND BALKAN WAR, 1913

Bulgaria's resentment over its share of the Turkish spoils at the end of the First Balkan War makes conflict with its former allies Greece and Serbia almost inevitable. Bulgaria's main war aim is to take control of the whole of Macedonia; against the urging of his advisors, King Ferdinand of Bulgaria orders his field armies to attack the Greek and Serbian forces in Macedonia. At the same time, Romania – which remained neutral in the first conflict – warns King Ferdinand that it will not stand aside from any new war. Montenegro announces that it will support its Serbian ally, and on 1 June Greece and Serbia also sign a treaty of mutual defence.

30 June Fighting begins, as the Bulgarians commit their five field armies totalling 360,000 men. They face in Macedonia nine Greek divisions with a total strength of 121,000, and the 300,000 men of the Serbian First, Second and Third Armies.

30 June–4 July Bulgarian Second Army, with something between 80,000 and 108,000 men (though its commander claimed he only had 36,000, and 20,000 of them untrained), defend the **Kilkis-Lahanas** line against a 177,860-strong Greek army. Each side has about 175 field guns, with the Bulgarians using much captured Ottoman artillery. The Greeks attack and capture the Bulgarian positions, killing some 6,000 men and capturing another 6,000 and 130 guns, for Greek losses of about 8,000.

30 June–8 July Battle of the **Bregalnitsa** river, between the recently formed and poorly trained Bulgarian Fourth Army and the Serbian First and Third Armies. The initial Bulgarian advance is halted, and the Serbs push them back across the river. Orders from the capital, Sofia, for the Bulgarian Fifth Army to support the Fourth arrive too late. Both sides suffer heavy casualties – about 20,000 Bulgarians, and 16,620 Serbs including 3,000 dead.

5 July Romania mobilizes its army, and Greece formally declares war on Bulgaria.

6 July Serbia formally declares war on Bulgaria.

10 July Romania declares war on Bulgaria, and sends 80,000 troops across the border to take the disputed Dobrudzha region.

12 July The Ottoman Empire declares war on Bulgaria, and troops advance into Thrace.

13 July Bulgaria sues for peace.

14 July 250,000 Romanian troops cross the Danube into undefended Bulgarian territory and quickly advance to the outskirts of Sofia.

18 July Units of Serbian Third Army with Montenegrin support attack Bulgarian defences at **Kalimantsi**, but are repeatedly thrown back.

This rare Bulgarian success stiffens determination to continue to resist the Serbians and Greeks.

22 July Ottoman troops reoccupy Adrianople and Eastern Thrace without meeting Bulgarian resistance. Romania agrees an armistice with Bulgaria.

29–30 July Battle of **Kresna Gorge**. As the Bulgarians retreat across their pre-war frontier, they turn and face tired and logistically over-extended Greek forces pursuing them, trap them in a narrow defile, and then reinforce this success. King Constantine – in the field as Greek C-in-C – argues for continuing the fight, but in reality all sides are war-weary, and an armistice is quickly agreed between the belligerent parties.

30 July Treaty of Bucharest is signed; this is followed by a separate peace treaty between Bulgaria and the Ottoman Empire, concluded at Constantinople.

Although much shorter than the First, the Second Balkan War has been no less costly. Bulgaria has suffered a further 93,000 dead and wounded; Greece, 5,851 killed and 23,847 wounded; and Serbia, 9,000 dead and 36,000 wounded. Although Montenegro's participation has been minor it has still suffered another 1,200 killed and wounded.

During the two wars together, diseases such as cholera and typhus have been responsible for heavy losses amongst the combatants; the total deaths from this cause are estimated at more than 126,000, with the Ottoman Turks alone losing 75,000 men to sickness during the First Balkan War.

* * *

The victors in the Balkan Wars gained new territory and enlarged their populations. The Greeks increased their territory by fully 68 per cent, and the Montenegrins by 62 per cent; Serbia almost doubled its territory, and Romania made a more modest gain of 5 per cent. Bulgaria – although the loser in the Second Balkan War – still made an overall gain of 16 per cent over the territory it had controlled before 1912.

Most of the combatant states were dissatisfied with their gains, and disputes over their grievances were to spill over into the Great War. Serbia,

Ottoman officers in discussion while their soldiers rest; the original caption – 'Turkish soldiers in the field 1912–1913' – gives no indication as to the date or location. Since all the men visible are wearing the pre-1909 dark blue uniform the photograph was probably taken just before or in the early days of the war. Two of the four officers have transverse shoulder straps of rank, suggesting that they belong to the infantry Gendarmerie. The stacked rifles are 7.65mm M1890 Turkish Mausers.

Ottoman Army buglers practising their calls. They wear khaki M1909 uniforms with woollen puttees and army-issue shoes, and have German-pattern belts and ammunition pouches. Their short fezzes appear to be a mixture of old red and new khaki-coloured types.

having made considerable gains on its southern borders, now looked to the north and the Austro-Hungarian province of Bosnia-Herzegovina. Notoriously, on 28 June 1914 Serbia's dispute with the Austrians over this region provoked the assassination in Sarajevo of the Austrian Archduke Franz Ferdinand, thus igniting the touchpaper that detonated World War I in early August.

The Ottoman Empire's humiliation was to lead to its siding during the Great War with the Central Powers (Germany and Austria-Hungary), alongside its enemy of only a year before, Bulgaria. Serbia and Montenegro sided with the Entente nations. Greece would remain fundamentally divided in sentiment between a neutralist king and a pro-Entente government; and Romania would reserve its options until mid-1916, before declaring war on Austria-Hungary.

THE ARMIES

The Ottoman Army, 1912–13

As a whole, the Ottoman Army in 1912 was a seasoned force that had been involved in fighting against an increasing number of rebellions in both its European and Asian possessions. Its peacetime strength was 280,000 men, which could be increased by wartime mobilization to more than 700,000 if necessary. Ottoman Army service was in four tiers. Recruits served for three years in the regular army (*nizam*), followed by six years in the army reserve (*ihtiad*). Next came a nine-year stint in the local reserve (*rediff*), and finally seven years as a local volunteer or *myustehafaz*. There were many exemptions from military service, and very few recruits served for the full 26 years.

About half of the Ottoman Army was stationed in Europe at the start of the First Balkan War. The three armies that made up the Western Army (or army group) in Macedonia were entirely composed of local reserve or *rediff* divisions. They were the Vardar Army with five divisions, the Macedonia Army with four, and the Salonika Army with three divisions. This isolated army group was to receive no reinforcements during the wars. The Eastern Army defending Thrace was divided in two: the First Eastern Army/ South, with I, II and IV Army Corps and one cavalry division; and Second Eastern Army/ North, with III, XVII and XVIII Army Corps.

The Ottoman regular army was well trained, motivated and equipped, but its heavy reliance on the less well trained and poorly equipped *rediff* local reserve formations was to prove its downfall in 1912–13. When the First Balkan War broke out the Ottoman troops in the field in Europe totalled almost 337,000 officers and men. Out of this total, 293,206 men were assigned to the four armies, of which 115,000 – including local garrison troops – were in Thrace. The remaining 200,000 men, including garrison troops, were in Macedonia, where they faced combined Balkan League forces of about 397,000 men.

Ottoman plans to transport large numbers of reinforcements from their armies in Syria and Palestine were thwarted by the presence of the Greek Navy in the Mediterranean. Because some Turkish soldiers had been demobilized just before the outbreak of the war, the Ottoman divisions in Europe were not always up to strength. The official establishment of an infantry division was built upon three 2,500-strong regiments, each with three battalions of 800 men. A battalion (*tabor*) was made up of four 200-man companies, each divided into four 50-strong platoons. In theory each infantry division should also have had a 24-gun artillery regiment.

This Bulgarian cavalry officer – whose shoulder boards seem, under magnification, to identify him as a lieutenant-colonel – leads troopers who are wearing a typical mixture of old coloured and new drab brown tunics. The officer is well mounted, but a shortage of good cavalry horses was to be a problem for the Bulgarian Army. At the outbreak of the First Balkan War they had 48 cavalry squadrons, but due to the static nature of much of the fighting they were often employed in the infantry role.

The Bulgarian Army, 1912–13

The Bulgarian Army was the largest and best-equipped of the Balkan League armies in 1912; it quickly expanded upon mobilization, from a peacetime strength of 60,000 to some 350,000 men. Although the Bulgarians had no recent experience of warfare the army was described by foreign military observers as being well motivated, and its soldiers were more than ready for war with the Ottoman Empire. It had a well-organized command structure, with a general staff and a very effective high command.

The Bulgarian military system, like most others, was divided into tiers by age. The First-Line Active Army (*Deystuuyushta Armiya*) took recruits aged between 21 and 23. This peacetime regular army had 2,891 officers, 4,204 NCOs and 54,872 men. Out of this total, 46,445 were considered as fully trained and equipped and combat-ready. The Second-Line Reserve Army (*Reserva Armiya*) was composed of former regulars between

This fighter festooned with cartridge belts is Gagergin Njdeh, one of the two leaders of the large Armenian company that volunteered to serve in the Macedonian-Adrianopolitan Volunteer Corps alongside the Bulgarian Army.

Crown Prince Constantine of Greece (left foreground, surrounded by ADCs and staff officers) commanded his father's armies in the field during the Balkan Wars. He was a headstrong commander; in autumn 1912 his wish to destroy the remaining Ottoman armies in front of his Greek forces was vetoed by Prime Minister Venizelos, who judged the capture of the city of Salonika in Macedonia – just before the arrival of Bulgarian troops – to be more important than the destruction of an already defeated enemy. Again, at the end of the Second Balkan War he failed to recognize the true plight of his over-extended army surrounded in the Kresna Gorge. Constantine succeeded to the throne in that year, at the age of 45, on the death of King George I.

24 and 40 years old. The two-tier National Militia (*Narodno Opolcenie*) accepted men aged from 41 to 44 in the Third Line, and aged 45 and 46 in the Fourth Line.

In September 1912 the mobilized army was organized into ten infantry divisions varying in size from 23,597 to 37,335 men. The typical division had a 'square' structure of two brigades, each of two regiments (*c*.4,580 men), each of two battalions (*c*.1,050 men). The three numbered main field armies had strengths of 94,875 all ranks (First Army), 96,568 (Second) and 111,363 (Third Army). In addition, there were two smaller formations: the Second Allied Army (37,335 men); and the 36,158-strong 2nd Infantry Division, which was divided into the Rhodope and Haskovo Detachments.

A cavalry formation was attached to each army. That of the First Army was designated a division, although of only brigade strength, with 2,241 all ranks. The Second Army's cavalry brigade had four regiments, and the Third Army's had three. Seven of the ten infantry divisions each had an artillery brigade with 72 guns, of which 36 were older pieces and 36 new quick-firing guns. The other three divisions in 1912 had either a weaker artillery brigade or a strengthened artillery regiment.

The Bulgarian Army had a number of elite 'patron regiments', each named after a member of the royal family, and distinguished by individually coloured collars, cuffs and hatbands (see Plate C2). There were ten 'patron' infantry regiments, four cavalry regiments and two artillery regiments. These units were not concentrated in a separate formation but were distributed amongst the divisions.

The Macedonian-Adrianopolitan Volunteer Corps, 1912–13

Volunteers for the army also came from Bulgarian Orthodox Christian communities in Ottoman-ruled Macedonia and Thrace. These were either taken into regular army units, or in this one case formed a separate volunteer corps – one of the largest and best-organized of the volunteer

elements of the Balkan Wars. The Macedonian-Adrianopolitan Volunteer Corps, with 14,670 men, was formed on 23 September 1912. It served in the First Balkan War against the Ottoman Turks, and in the Second War against the Serbians, before being disbanded in October 1913. It was seen by some Europeans as a liberation force, and it attracted international volunteers totalling 531 men, including 82 Russians, 40 Serbs, 68 Romanians, 21 volunteers from Austria-Hungary, 12 Montenegrins and 3 Greeks, plus single volunteers from Albania, Persia, Italy and England. A company-sized Armenian 'legion' of 275 men was also inorporated in the MAVC, commanded by two well-known nationalists, Gagergin Njdeh and Andranik Toros Ozanian. The Armenians felt common cause with the Bulgarians, being willing to fight for anyone who opposed the Ottoman Turks.

Arms and equipment for the MAVC came from Bulgarian Army stores, and most of the volunteers were armed with Russian-made Berdan bolt-action rifles. Although a brown uniform did exist for the Corps, many volunteers wore civilian clothing. The official uniform had green collar, cuffs, and shoulder straps, with the unit number painted in gold Roman numerals on the latter. Headgear was usually a black fur hat with the unit's brass cap badge on the front, but this was also seen on other types of hat (see Plate C3).

The Greek Army, 1912–13

Greece had a small peacetime regular army of 3,802 officers and 18,875 men, which could be increased upon mobilization to 110,000 all ranks. There was also a National Guard with 80,000 men, and the National Guard Reserve with an additional 60,000 men. More men could have been called up, but the Greeks were limited by the stores of clothing, equipment and weapons available for volunteers. Greek recruits were expected to serve for a total of 31 years –

Three Serbian cavalry troopers, pictured outside their barracks during the Balkan Wars. In the original colour-tinted image they are wearing light blue *sajcaka* caps and double-breasted tunics, with black collar patches, red breeches and black riding boots. They hold the enlisted ranks' sabre; Serbian cavalry were usually armed with the Mauser M1899 or M1899/07 carbine, or the more modern M1910.

two in the Active Army, 21 years in the First Reserve and eight in the Second Reserve.

A French military mission that arrived in Greece in 1911 under Gen Eydoux encouraged the Greeks to move to a 'triangular' infantry division with three infantry regiments of three battalions, plus two artillery battalions and a half-company of cavalry for reconnaissance. This new system left a surplus of infantry regiments, which were formed into additional infantry divisions upon mobilization.

The army was divided into two main field armies: the Army of Thessaly under the command of Crown Prince Constantine, and the Army of Epirus under LtGen Konstantinos Sapountzakis. The 100,000-strong Army of Thessaly comprised seven infantry divisions, four independent battalions of *Evzones* (elite light infantry recruited in mountain areas), a cavalry brigade and various support units, with 70 machine guns and 120 artillery pieces. The Army of Epirus was a much smaller 10,000-man division-sized formation, with eight infantry battalions, one Evzone battalion, a cavalry company and 24 field guns. It was reinforced during the war by various volunteer units including the Cretan volunteer regiment and the Italian Legion or '*Garibaldini*' (*see* below).

The Greeks also received volunteers for the regular army from the Greek populations in Macedonia and Epirus. Macedonians in the regular Greek Army served mainly in the so-called 'Holy Regiment'. According to orders of battle, the Army of Epirus included nine small Macedonian scout 'corps' with a total of 1,812 men, and nine even smaller Epirot scout platoons totalling 446 men. The Greeks also received volunteers from abroad, including a company of Greek emigrants from New York.

Cretan volunteers, 1912–13

After a series of rebellions against the Ottoman rulers from 1860 onwards, the island of Crete had been given the status of an autonomous state by international treaty since 1898. Prince George of Greece was installed as the head of the new state, until his replacement in 1906 by a local politician, Alexandros Zaimis. Crete formally announced its union with Greece in 1908, but this was not recognized by the international community until after the Balkan Wars in December 1913.

The island had its own military force in the form of a Gendarmerie, with a strength of 1,466 all ranks at the outbreak of the Balkan Wars. This militarized police force had been well trained by Italian instructors and had a reputation for reliability. The Gendarmerie were sent by the Cretan government to assist their fellow Greeks at the outbreak of the First Balkan War, and were given the task of policing the newly captured city of Salonika by the Greek Army. The gendarmes wore a distinctive black uniform comprising a tight-fitting jacket with white Italian-style

A Montenegrin hilltop trench facing an Ottoman attack during the winter of 1912/13. In the foreground is the battalion standard-bearer, wearing an army-issue cloak around his shoulders; his comrades have a variety of winter clothing, including several sheepskin cloaks. All are armed with the Russian Mosin-Nagant M1891, the standard rifle in service with the Montenegrin Army in 1912.

Romanian artillerymen man a German 7.5cm Krupp M1903 field gun during field manoeuvres. Before the introduction of the M1912 grey-green uniform, artillerymen wore dark blue field caps, brown double-breasted tunics with dark blue collars and pointed cuffs, and grey trousers with red piping. The same shade of piping seems to be evident on the caps and tunics in this photograph.

collar, pantaloon trousers worn with a blue sash, and a round black *toca* hat. The cap badge was red with a silver anchor device for Crete, below the superimposed monogram of Greek Crown Prince George II.

Cretans also volunteered in large numbers to serve in the Greek regular army, usually in their own distinct units. The Army of Epirus included an 'Independent Cretans Regiment', and other units mentioned in orders of battle include the 'Students Sacred Band' and the 'Cretans Military Company'. Volunteers from Crete were also formed into so-called 'scout corps', *ad hoc* platoons of less than 50 men; Cretans formed 77 of these, with a total establishment of 3,556 men. These scouts wore regular Greek Army uniforms without any unit distinctions apart from a cross on their breast pocket. However, some Cretan volunteers with Greek officers were photographed wearing their traditional dress with distinctive *sarikia* headscarves.

The Italian Legion, 1912–13

During Greece's unsuccessful war against the Ottoman Turks in 1897, a volunteer unit recruited from the famous Italian revolutionary group, the Garibaldini, had played an important part, fighting at the battle of Dhomokos. (Volunteers from this movement, one of the driving forces behind the unification of Italy in the 1860s, had gone on to fight in a number of wars of liberation in South America and Europe during the later 19th century.) In 1912 some of the survivors of the 1897 war volunteered with their sons and other younger volunteers to fight for Greece once again. The 800-strong Italian Legion arrived in Greece with seven members of the Garibaldi family in its ranks, and commanded by Guiseppe Garibaldi's son Ricciotti. The Legion fought in a mixed formation of light troops that also included Cretan volunteers and Greek Evzones. They were present at a number of engagements, culminating in the siege of Janina in November 1912, before returning to Italy at the end of the First Balkan War. Although pictured at the start of the war in their famous red shirts, they were reported to have been issued with red-dyed Greek Army tunics and caps before they went into the front lines (see Plate G4).

The Serbian Army 1912–13

Serbia had fought a number of conflicts in the late 19th century, and its soldiers had a reputation as hard fighters. After 1906 a modernization programme had been introduced, and by 1912 the regular army was well equipped and trained. The Serbian military structure was divided into four tiers, with the First to Third levels called '*Bans*' and differentiated by age. The First *Ban* (I Ban) was made up of men aged from 21 to 31, the II Ban of men between 32 and 38 years, and the III Ban (the *Poskana Odbrana*) from men between the ages of 39 and 45 years. There was an additional fourth level, a militia force formed from men too young or too old for I–III Ban service – volunteers aged between 17 and 20, or 45 and 50 years.

In a pre-war photograph, two Bulgarian irregular volunteers strike heroic poses in Macedonian woodland. They had operated here against Ottoman forces for decades; although it is difficult to date such photographs, the large-calibre breech-loading rifles suggest the turn of the century. Men like these fought alongside the Bulgarian Army in 1912 and again in 1913.

Resting in the street of a Turkish-held town, these men are Albanian auxiliaries of the Ottoman Army. Albanians of various religious backgrounds fought on several sides during the Balkan Wars, although the majority under arms were fighting for the Ottomans. These men are all wearing at least some items of military uniform, and look in many ways like typical Ottoman *rediff* troops apart from their distinctive white Albanian hats. They are armed with short M1893 rifles.

The Serbian Army had a peacetime strength of 3,700 officers and 165,000 men in five infantry divisions, each of two brigades, each with two regiments. It was increased on mobilization to a force of 336,348 all ranks in 15 infantry divisions, with an additional ten divisions formed from II and III Ban reservists. A Serbian division was 23,500 strong, comprising four regiments of 4,860 men, each having four battalions of 1,116 men. The battalions had four 260-man companies, each divided into four 60-man platoons, in four 15-man sections.

The Serbian Army in the field in 1912 was divided into the First Army under the command of Crown Prince Alexander, with 132,000 men; the Second Army with 74,000 men; and the Third Army with 76,000 men. Two smaller forces – the Ibor Army, with 25,000 men, and the Javor Brigade, with 12,000 – completed the total.

The Montenegrin Army, 1912–13

The Montenegrin Army (*Crnagorska Vojska*) defended a tiny nation of about 250,000 people by means of a militia system that mobilized most of the male population. All men between the ages of 18 and 62 were liable for military service, and the Montenegrin Army had a mobilized strength of about 40,000. Recruits aged from 18 to 19 were given 12 months' basic training before joining the rest of the soldiers aged between 20 and 53. A second-line reserve force (*Narodna Vojska*) took the older recruits, between the ages of 53 and 62.

The army was divided into three field forces of different sizes. The Coastal Force (8,000 men, commanded by Gen Martinovic) had three brigades; Zeta Force (15,000 men, under Crown Prince Danilo) had five brigades; and the Eastern Force (12,600 men, led by Gen Vukotic) had four brigades. The Montenegrin brigade was a flexible formation; each might have anything between four and ten infantry battalions, and each battalion four or five clan-based companies, each with five platoons. A total artillery of 126 pieces had mainly light mountain guns with a handful of heavier field pieces. These were divided between the field forces: two field and two heavy batteries in Zeta Force, and one of each in the Coastal and Eastern Forces. In the mountainous terrain in which the Montenegrins operated there was no real need for mounted troops, although they did have a token element of 30 cavalrymen and one officer. During the war volunteers for the Montenegrin Army came from several sources, including returning emigrants from the USA, and from the Slavic population of the Austro-Hungarian Empire.

Because Montenegro had no direct quarrel with Bulgaria, its participation in the Second Balkan War was limited to one division, of 12,800 men in three brigades. This contingent joined the Serbian Third Army on campaign.

As individual fighters the Montenegrins were formidable foes, but their experience lay in small-unit irregular tactics that had not really prepared them for modern warfare. Having no official medical corps, and only a single 28-bed military hospital, they had to rely on local and foreign Red Cross volunteers.

Pre-war photograph of a machine gun squad of a Bulgarian Army 'patron regiment' with their M1908 Maxims. The carriages have wheels fitted, allowing them to be pushed forwards when the stands are folded up. Although the original caption does not specify the regiment, the white cap band and other facings suggest the 6th Infantry Regiment (HRH King Ferdinand's).

The Romanian Army, 1913

In 1913 the Romanian Army was the largest regular service in the Balkans, with a peacetime strength of 6,149 officers and 94,170 other ranks. This could be more than quadrupled upon mobilization, to 10,000 officers and 460,000 men, in 247 infantry battalions and 93 cavalry squadrons. There were 180 batteries of medium artillery; 180 machine guns were reported, but may not have arrived in time for use in 1913.

The army structure was divided into the familiar three tiers. The First-Line Active Army (*Armata Activa*) took men between the ages of 21 and 23; the Second-Line Reserve Army (*Reserva Armatei*) was composed of men between 29 and 40; and those aged from 41 to 46 served in the Third-Line Militia (*Militii*).

During the Second Balkan War the Romanians mobilized 330,000 men, divided between two main operational forces, by far the more important being the Main Operations Army with four army corps. These I to IV Corps were made up of eight Active divisions and two Reserve divisions, plus two cavalry divisions. A second major force, the Dobrudzha Corps or V Corps, comprised two Active and one Reserve division. A division (27,000 men) had two Active and one Reserve brigade, and brigades comprised two regiments (*c.*4,800 men) each of three battalions more than 1,100 strong.

The 80,000-strong Dobrudzha Corps was given the task of occupying the southern Dobrudzha, while the 250,000-man Main Operations Army was to advance into Bulgaria with Sofia as its objective. Since the Bulgarian Army was tied down fighting the Serbs and Greeks the Romanians were able to advance without any real opposition, and had reached the outskirts of the Bulgarian capital by the time the peace agreement ended the Second Balkan War.

Bulgarian artillerymen prepare to bring their German 7.5cm Krupp M1886 guns into action during the siege of Adrianople. The M1886 was an older, slow-firing piece, and by 1912 it was being relegated to the newly formed 2nd Artillery Regiment, which distributed sub-units among the infantry divisions. Most of the crews are wearing the grey greatcoat. Under magnification, one of the men in the foreground can be seen to have a gold monogram device on his shoulder strap, suggesting that he belongs to either the 3rd or 4th Artillery Regiments, which were both elite 'patron' units.

Macedonian irregulars, 1912–13

Ottoman-ruled Macedonia in 1912 was divided into five provinces, with populations deeply divided by religious tradition as much as by 'nationality'. Macedonians who followed the Greek Orthodox church were regarded as Greeks, and those who followed the Bulgarian Orthodox church as Bulgarians. The same applied to the smaller numbers who followed the Serbian Orthodox liturgy, who were therefore regarded as Serbs. When serious resistance to Ottoman Turkish rule began in the 19th cntury, the armed bands that fought the Turks were also divided along religious lines. Bulgarian, Greek and Serbian nationalist groups or 'committees' raised their own armed units, who fought against each other almost as often as against the Ottoman Army. Each of these various groups was fighting for Macedonia to be incorporated into its own motherland, whether that be Greece, Bulgaria or Serbia.

An alternative to this divisive chaos was offered by the Internal Macedonian Revolutionary Organization (IMRO) formed in Salonika in 1893. IMRO was created by a group of intellectuals who argued for an autonomous Macedonia within the Ottoman Empire. Although claiming to represent all Macedonians, IMRO was in fact dominated by Bulgarian Macedonians. They formed armed groups or *chetas* of between 15 and 50 men, who fought a bitter guerrilla war against the Ottoman Army in the late 1890s. A large-scale rebellion by IMRO and pro-Bulgarian bands in 1903 was put down ruthlessly by 175,000 Ottoman troops. This defeat of the IMRO *chetas* left the field open for the diverse nationalist groups to dominate the war against the Ottoman Empire, and by 1907 there were about 110 Bulgarian, 30 Serbian and 80 Greek armed bands active in Macedonia. There were even reported to be eight Romanian bands fighting in the region, trying to establish their own claims to part of Macedonia's territory.

A Serbian artillery piece dug into a firing position in the hills surrounding the Ottoman-held city of Adrianople. At the request of her ally Bulgaria, Serbia sent a force of 47,000 men and 72 guns to help in the siege. The Serbians paid a heavy price, losing about 8,000 men during the assaults on this strategically vital fortress.

When the First Balkan War broke out these armed groups, which had been largely subdued by the Ottomans, were ready to fight again. Forty-four Bulgarian *chetas* were operating in 1912, attacking Ottoman units and disrupting their movements. Greek Macedonians, known as *Makedonimachoi* or 'Macedonian fighters', fought in support of the Greek Army in 1912. In the early years of the century they had been trained by seconded Greek Army officers and supplied with French M1874 Gras rifles. The Serbian population of Macedonia also had irregular units fighting in the part of the region bordering Serbia in 1912. Under the title of Serbian *Narodna Odbrana*, 'National Defence', these guerrillas operated in support of the Serbian Army.

Albanian volunteers, 1912–13

The people of Albania were divided along tribal and religious lines, but the majority of the population were of the Muslim faith. Many Muslim Albanians volunteered to fight for the Ottoman Army as second-line troops, since they preferred rule by their Turkish co-religionists to any possible domination by the Christian Orthodox Serbs, Bulgarians or Greeks. Ottoman garrisons in Albania were often supplemented by local volunteers, who were presumably armed and equipped with what little the Turks had available.

Conversely, Albanian Catholics or 'Malisorri' who lived in the north and west of the country volunteered to fight for the undermanned Montenegrin Army. Altogether there were an estimated 6,000 of them serving as irregulars with the Montenegrins by the end of the war. Meanwhile, yet other Albanians fought for an independent state, and had no intention of swapping Ottoman rule for domination by any of the Balkan League nations.

A mountain battery of the Montenegrin Army assembles at Tzrminitza at the start of the First Balkan War. Although not visible in this cropped photograph, this battery has four mountain guns and four Maxim machine guns. Most of Montenegro's 150-odd artillery pieces were gifts from Italy and Russia. All the artillerymen here are kitted out in regular khaki uniforms, with the *kapitza* pillbox cap based on traditional headgear; the two officers in the foreground are wearing the peaked cap introduced by the 1910 regulations.

WEAPONS & EQUIPMENT

Small arms

Revolvers in service with the combatants in the Balkan Wars included the Austrian Gasser, widely used by the Montenegrins and Serbians in various models produced between 1870 and 1882. The Serbians also used the Russian M1891 Nagant and the M1870 Francotte. Bulgaria used the Russian version of the Smith & Wesson M1880 revolver, and the 1906 and 1908 Parabellum ('Luger') semi-automatic pistols. Having ordered 1,500 of the latter in 1908, Bulgaria placed an order for 10,000 more in 1912. Greece used the French St Etienne M1874 revolver amongst others, and the Ottomans the Mauser C96 'broomhandle' semi-automatic pistol and the FN-Browning M1903. Other handguns in service during the wars included the Browning 1900 and Mannlicher 1903 pistols.

As might be expected with so many nations involved, a wide variety of rifles saw service in 1912–13. The Ottoman Army in 1912 had a shortfall in small arms, with only 713,404 rifles of all types on hand for its million-plus infantrymen. Both of the main Ottoman armies in the Balkan theatre were critically short of rifles, with an estimated 20 per cent of troops unarmed. This meant that obsolete types had to be employed alongside the modern Mauser M1890 and M1903, including large numbers of M1874 Peabody-Martinis, and even older British Sniders. Carbines for the cavalry were also in short supply, and many Turkish cavalrymen had to make do with unwieldy rifles.

Bulgaria used two main models of Austrian 8mm Mannlichers, the M1880/90 and the M1895, in both rifle and carbine form. They had 343,428 rifles in service at the start of the war, and during the conflict ·these were supplemented by imports of 50,000 Russian M1891s. Russia

also sent a gift of 25,000 M1870 'Berdan II' rifles to supplement those already in use by Bulgarian second-line troops; this weapon had a Mauser-type bolt action, and was made at the Tula arsenal. Some Bulgarian reserve troops were also armed with the Russian M1869 Krnka, a breech-loading conversion of the British Snider that shared the weaknesses of the similar French 'tabatière'. This type had been sold to the public after being withdrawn from army service, so volunteers would have brought their own with them.

Among its c.190,000 weapons the Greek Army used the Austrian 6.5mm rotary-magazine Mannlicher-Schönauer M1907 in rifle and carbine forms, as well as large numbers of the M1874 Gras to equip reserve and militia units.

Serbia's most modern rifle was the 7mm Mauser M1910, but the Serbians also had earlier M1899 and M1899/07 models. They converted about 45,000 single-shot Mauser-Koka M1880s into magazine rifles; designated M1880/07, these were issued to second-line units. Among their total of 288,000 weapons the Serbians also had unconverted Mauser-Koka M1884 carbines.

Montenegro had purchased 20,000 Russian Mosin-Nagant M1891 rifles in 1898, and ordered another 20,000 in 1905. These were used alongside earlier types bought in the late 1800s, including the Austrian Werndl M1873 and Greek Gras M1874. The reserve troops were equipped with 30,000 Russian M1870 Berdan rifles, as also used by the Serbs and Bulgarians.

The Romanian Army used the Mannlicher M1893 as its first-line rifle and carbine in 1913, and had also imported 50,000 Steyr M1912 rifles in 1912. At the last minute they also bought from Austria-Hungary 60,000 M1890 and M1895 8mm Mannlichers. Some Romanian reserve troops were armed with the Peabody-Martini M1879 manufactured under licence by OEWG in Austria.

(continued on page 33)

Posing against a carpet backdrop in an improvised photographic studio in the field, this Ottoman soldier wears the typical uniform of a *rediff* local reservist – the old red fez with blue tassel, the M1893 dark blue uniform, thick woollen leggings tucked into socks, and a pair of peasant shoes. He is in little danger of running out of ammunition, with at least four and perhaps five bandoliers of clips for his M1890 Mauser.

RIGHT **In a carefully posed photograph, Ottoman troops 'defend their position' at the battle of Kumanovo in October 1912. All the rankers are wearing M1909 uniforms in various shades of khaki, with what appears to be a mixture of khaki and red fezzes. The man lying in the foreground may be a civilian volunteer, since he has added a large star-and-crescent insignia to his hat to show his allegiance. The ammunition pouches are of German pattern, as was most Ottoman Army equipment in 1912–13; large shipments were imported after 1909.**

OTTOMAN ARMY

1: *Nizam* regular infantryman, 1912
2: *Rediff* reservist infantryman, Kırmastı Regt, 1912
3: Trooper, regular cavalry; Adrianople, 1913

A

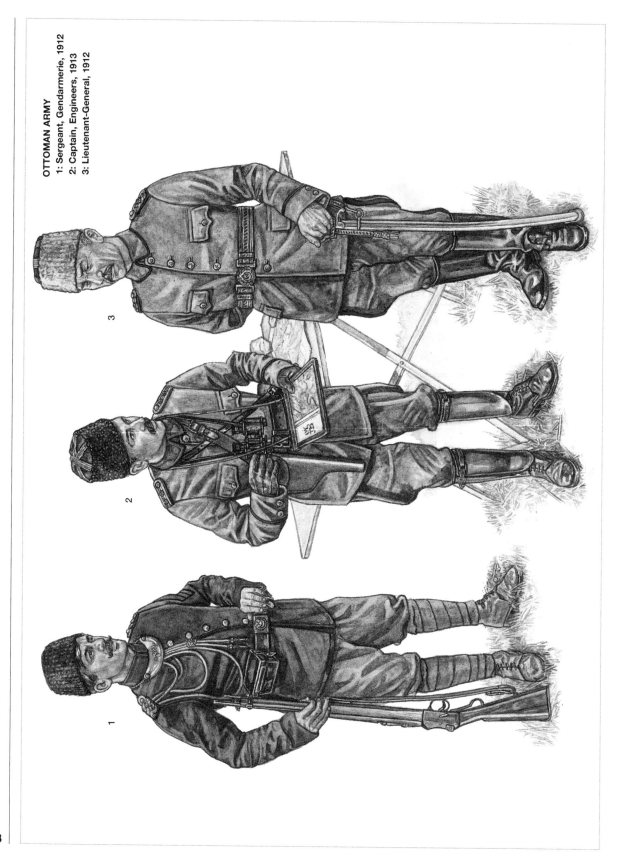

OTTOMAN ARMY
1: Sergeant, Gendarmerie, 1912
2: Captain, Engineers, 1913
3: Lieutenant-General, 1912

B

BULGARIAN ARMY
1: Captain, 10th Infantry Regiment, 1912
2: Second lieutenant, 2nd Artillery Regt, 1913
3: Volunteer, Macedonian-Adrianopolitan Vol Corps, 1912

C

D

ROMANIAN & MONTENEGRIN ARMIES
1: Private, Romanian 7th Reserve Inf Regt, 1913
2: Corporal, Romanian 16th Inf Regt, 1913
3: Montenegrin standard-bearer, 9th Durmitorska Bde, 1912
4: Corporal, Montenegrin infantry, 1912

E

SERBIAN ARMY

1: Private, 6th Inf Regt, Drina Division, 1912
2: Infantryman, II Ban, 1912
3: Captain, 4th Hvy Artillery Bty, Third Army, 1913
4: Volunteer, III Ban, 1912

GREEK ARMY

1: Sergeant, 7th Evzones Battalion, 1912
2: Captain, Engineers, 1913
3: Private, 4th Infantry Regiment, 1912
4: Volunteer, Italian Legion, 1912

IRREGULAR VOLUNTEERS
1: Greek monastery guard; Mount Athos, 1913
2: *Makedonimachoi* fighter; Macedonia, 1912
3: Albanian *Malisorri* auxiliary, Montenegrin Army, 1912

H

Two Bulgarian soldiers of the 27th Infantry Regiment, which was based in the south of the country, pose for a photograph before leaving for the front. Both wear rather roughly-made versions of the tobacco-brown tunic with red collar, cuffs and shoulder straps, the latter bearing the metal Roman numerals '27'. Like many Bulgarian soldiers, both have *tsarvuli* peasant shoes instead of army boots. Note that for the camera both have opened their single belt pouches and have arranged clips for their Mannlicher M1880/90 rifles in a visible display.

Machine guns

The value of machine guns had been fully recognized by 1912, and all the armies in the Balkan Wars used as many as they could acquire; but machine guns were expensive, and relatively few were in service when the wars began.

The exact number of machine guns in service with the Ottoman Army is difficult to assess, since sources are contradictory. Estimates vary between 388 and 556 guns, although the larger figure probably includes all those in service throughout the Ottoman Empire. The estimate of 388 is based on figures which show that the Second Eastern Army in Thrace had 23 machine-gun detachments with four guns each, and the Western Army in Albania and Macedonia had 19 four-gun detachments.

These were mainly equipped with German M1909 Maxims, but it is probable that some French Hotchkiss guns were also in service.

The Bulgarians had imported 144 Maxim M1908 guns in 1908, allocating four to each infantry regiment, and had 232 Maxims by 1913. Greece had only 84 Austro-Hungarian Schwarzlose M1907 guns when the war began, though also a number of light machine guns. Serbia used the Maxim DWM M1909, and had 230 in service during the conflict.

Montenegro, with the smallest army, had only 12 Maxim machine guns in 1912, as well as another seven 'older' guns that may have been Nordenfeldts. During the course of the war the Montenegrins ordered a further 50 Maxims, but these may not have arrived in time to be used. The employment of machine guns by the Romanians in 1913 is uncertain, although they had recently imported 130 Maxim and Schwarzlose models.

Artillery

Most of the combatants were reasonably well equipped with modern field guns, though obsolete types dating back to the 1870s were still in evidence.

The Ottoman Army's modern field guns included 648 Krupp 7.5cm M1904s and 88 M1910s. Modern heavier guns were in short supply, with only 18 Krupp 10.5cm Belagerungskanone and the same number of Krupp 15cm howitzers in service in 1912.

In total the Bulgarians had 1,108 artillery pieces, the vast majority of them being 75mm, including 324 French guns delivered in 1906–07. They did have 36 French 120mm M1907s, and 24 M1897 150mm Schneiders, as well as a number of 8.7cm and 7.5cm Krupp M1873 guns. Greece was short of all types of artillery but especially of heavier guns; the mainstay of the Greek artillery was the French 75mm field gun, of which 144 had been supplied after 1908. Serbia had a total of 544 guns, including 188 French 75mm quick-firers ordered in 1906, as well as

This Greek soldier wears M1908 summer walking-out uniform with an M1907 German-type service cap – this model was replaced during the Balkan Wars with the M1910. His cap badge is a rather dark shade, which might suggest that he is an artilleryman; however, some Greek soldiers wore non-regulation darker cap badges on privately purchased uniforms. The summer uniform was of the same cut as the winter version but was made from cotton instead of wool, and had no coloured distinctions.

RIGHT Greek artillerymen, posed with a 75mm French M1897 field gun, wear standard M1908 khaki campaign uniform, with the ammunition pouches that were particular to this branch and the cavalry. All have brown leather gaiters over the top of their laced ankle boots, apart from the man sitting at the left, who wears short marching boots. The officer (sitting second from right) and the men on either side of him have spurred boots. The three NCOs and the officer carry the M1868 artillery sword; several men have the French M1892 revolver, and gunners in the background are armed with the Mannlicher-Schönauer carbine.

some 90mm French M1877 field guns. Heavier types used by the Serbians were the 120mm French M1897 Schneider, and 24 heavy 150mm howitzers. Montenegro's artillery was a mixture of a few modern field guns and mortars with older types dating back to the 1870s and 1880s; its total of 150-odd pieces included a number of mountain guns and mortars supplied by the Italians and Russians. The modern types included eight 76.2mm M1902 field guns and six 76.2mm mountain guns, all from Russia. Heavier pieces included 16 guns of 120mm, of which six were British dating back to 1860.

The Romanians' medium field gun was the 7.5cm Krupp M1903, which had been supplied in batches up to 1908; they also used the 105mm Schneider M1910. Any other guns in service in 1913 were old recoiling-carriage types, and these were probably left in barracks when the Romanians invaded Bulgaria.

Military transport

At a time when motor transport was very much in its infancy all the armies in the Balkan Wars relied on large numbers of horses and oxen to pull their artillery and to transport men and supplies. The Bulgarians had a total of 28,000 horse- and ox-carts to move their supplies, and shortages of draught animals often slowed their advances in 1912. The Ottoman Army was also critically short of draught animals, and needed an influx of about 48,000 horses and oxen for their war needs. Such figures are not surprising given that it was estimated that each artillery regiment needed 400 animals to pull its guns and wagons. Human porters were also extensively employed by all armies in the Balkan Wars, and were especially useful in the mountainous terrain that covered most of the war fronts. When a large percentage of the able-bodied men were already in the army, then women were employed as porters.

Motor vehicles were used, but in very modest numbers. All the combatant armies had some staff cars, but were only just beginning to buy motor lorries. For instance, the Bulgarian Army – with a mobilized strength of nearly 600,000 men – had just 36 cars, 12 lorries and two motorcycles. There were some 150 private and government motor vehicles in the whole of Serbia in 1912, and those owned by civilians were requisitioned by the army. Of the total of about 300 motor vehicles in the whole of the Ottoman Empire only a handful were used in the Balkan Wars, and those mainly as staff cars.

Air arms

The use of aircraft by armies was at an even more embryo stage, having been pioneered by the Italians in the Italo-Turkish War in 1911, but most of the nations involved did have rudimentary air arms. The aircraft flown in the Balkans were a mixture of French Blériot XI, Nieuport and Deperdussin monoplanes, and Maurice Farman and Henri Farman

Detail from a group photograph of tough-looking Serbian 'I Ban' soldiers, wearing the M1908 uniform with slight variations to their dress. All wear the distinctive *sajcaka* cap. The officer (centre right) has high boots, one soldier low boots, and the two outside men *opanci* peasant shoes. Note the crossed suspender-straps for the belt pouches; the rifle is the most common type in service, the Serbian M1910 Mauser. The officer has a sabre, and a holstered handgun with a lanyard.

A Serbian second lieutenant of the 2nd Artillery Regiment poses in field uniform, 1912. His collar is in the black of the artillery branch, as are his shoulder boards, which display the silver Roman numeral '2' above his star of rank. The peakless cap is also piped in the branch colour, and he would have black piping down the outer seams of his breeches. He is well kitted out from a Belgrade officers' outfitters, with a leather map case and valise and a cloth-covered water canteen.

biplanes. The handful of aircraft on each side were flown by pioneering daredevils who had to invent techniques for reconnaissance and bombing as they went along. One of the Greek Army's pilots employed a bombing method that was courageous to the point of insanity, since it involved him flying over the enemy with grenades held between his knees. Because the grenades had very short fuses he had to fly only a few feet above the ground, throwing his missiles out of the cockpit while being shot at from close range.

The Serbian *Srpska Avijatika* had three aircraft at the start of the conflict, and a total of ten by the end of the Second Balkan War. The Serbs employed Russian pilots who brought several aircraft with them to the Balkans, and also flew them in support of the Montenegrins in Albania. Greece started off with four Maurice Farman MF-7s and during the war added two floatplanes to their inventory. Bulgaria began the war with five aircraft, but acquired a further 17 before 1913, thus ending up with the largest Balkan air arm. They flew a number of reconnaissance flights, bombing missions and leaflet-dropping flights during the First Balkan War, losing three planes to ground fire during the whole conflict; one Blériot XI pilot dropped hand grenades on the fortress of Adrianople in October 1912. Romania had formed an Aviation Group (*Grupul Aviatie*) in 1911, and by 1913 had four Henri Farmans and four Blériot XIs. The Romanians used some of their aircraft for an historic leaflet-dropping flight over the Bulgarian capital in 1913. This harmless propaganda mission to Sofia had historic significance, in that it was the first time that one European nation's aircraft had flown over an enemy's capital city.

The Ottoman Empire had first looked into setting up an air arm in 1909, but progress was slow, largely because of financial constraints. By 1912 ten Turkish pilots had received training in France, but they were still relatively inexperienced by the start of the First Balkan War. German pilots flew some of the Turkish aircraft on several reconnaissance missions in 1912, but by the Second Balkan War the Ottoman pilots were better prepared. Problems with friendly ground fire led to the adoption in March 1913 of red panels with white star-and-crescent insignia – the first recorded use of national markings on military aircraft.

UNIFORMS

With so many combatant forces involved, and such a wide variety of uniforms worn in each army, a comprehensive description of their dress is impossible in a publication of this size. However, a brief summary of the main uniforms, cross-referenced to specific examples in the colour

plates, will give an overall view of the clothing worn by the six armies and the various irregulars involved in the two conflicts.

The soldiers of the **Ottoman Army** wore both the newly introduced M1909 khaki uniform (Plate A1) with khaki cloth fez, and the M1893 dark blue uniform with red fez (Plate A2). Cavalry were photographed wearing the new *kabalak* headgear (Plate A3). Officers wore a grey-green uniform with the fez-shaped hat covered in lambswool (Plates B1 & B2).

Most **Bulgarian Army** infantrymen wore a 'tobacco-brown' uniform with peaked cap (Plate C1), while their officers wore a grey-green uniform (Plate D1). The 'patron regiments' wore their own distinctions on their uniforms (Plate C2), and were issued with the best-quality clothing available. When parade uniforms were phased out for the rest of the army in 1906 as a cost-cutting measure, the patron regiments had retained theirs. Shortages of all uniforms meant that officers would often mix items of older and dress uniforms with their more modern ones (Plate D2). Although the Bulgarians do not seem to have issued

As the Montenegrin Army had no staff structure, this officers' tent on the battlefield would serve as an headquarters. This group includes three princes of the royal family who all held high command in the army. At left centre ('1') is Prince Danilo, and right centre ('2') Prince Mirko; both wear the peaked cap with the new M1910 uniform. Cut by the right edge of the photo is Prince Petar, wearing the same green-khaki pillbox cap as most of the other officers.

BRANCH-OF-SERVICE COLOURS 1912–13

	Infantry	Cavalry	Artillery	Engineers	Medical	Gendarmes
Ottoman Army	none	Light grey	Dark blue	Blue	Red	Scarlet
Bulgarian Army	Red	Red	Black	Black	Black	*
Greek Army	Red	Purple	Madder	Blue	Red	Black
Serbian Army	Red	Dark blue	Black	Cherry-red	Brown	*
Montenegrin Army	Scarlet	*	Yellow	Green	*	*

* These branches did not exist in the armies indicated

A squad of *Dorobantzi* soldiers, of the Romanian second-line territorial reserve, pose together in a studio at the end of the Second Balkan War. They wear fleece hats with a hawk's feather, and cap badges featuring the king's cypher. As second-line troops they have typically mixed clothing: the dark blue M893 tunic, with grey-green trousers from the M1912 uniform. Some have woollen puttees, while others have their trousers tucked into the tops of their high-shaft laced ankle boots. (Courtesy Ablibris)

their second-line troops with late 19th-century uniforms systematically, like other Balkan armies, they did have to clothe some of their soldiers with older uniforms dating back to the 1870s.

The **Greek Army** in 1912 looked comparatively modern when compared to many other armies on the eve of World War I. Most soldiers wore the M1908 olive-khaki uniform with képi-style cap (Plate G3), which the Greeks were proud to say was one of the first khaki uniforms introduced following the British Army's example. Trousers were straight-legged, but were soon adapted for combat by the addition of puttees. Greek officers wore an olive-khaki képi and tunic, most wearing breeches instead of the enlisted ranks' trousers (Plate G2). Evzone light infantry wore their own highly distinctive uniforms (Plate G1), while some reserve troops and gendarmes wore the old M1896 uniform. For infantry this had a dark blue képi and tunic, usually worn with grey trousers with red-piped outer seams.

The standard uniform of the **Serbian Army** was the M1908 khaki uniform (Plates F1 & F3), which was worn by infantry and cavalry. 'Second Ban' troops wore a mixture of uniforms, but mainly the dark blue M1896 (Plate F2). Second-line cavalry wore the 1896 tunic in dark blue or light blue, with red trousers. 'Third Ban' soldiers wore civilian dress with the occasional military item (Plate F4).

Regular soldiers of the **Montenegrin Army** wore the M1910 khaki uniform (Plate E4), but many of their comrades had to make do with traditional civilian clothing (Plate E3). Officers wore a similar khaki uniform to their men, with either the *kapitza* pillbox cap or a peaked (visored) cap. The 100-strong Royal Bodyguard had their own distinctive light blue uniform, which was based on traditional dress.

The **Romanian Army** in 1913 wore a variety of uniforms, but most first-line troops had recently been issued with the grey-green M1912 (Plate E2). Many reserve soldiers still wore coloured uniforms dating back to the 1890s (Plate E1), or a mixture of the two. Reserve artillerymen and border guards wore brown tunics with the dark blue field cap or even the earlier képi. *Jagers* wore brown tunics with green facings, and a distinctive brimmed black hat with a green pompon at the front. *Grancieri* frontier guards wore dark blue tunics with *Pickelhaube* helmets, but these would soon be replaced in the field with the grey-green uniform.

Irregulars of all armies usually had to wear their own civilian clothing, but since this was often regionally distinctive it acted as a sort of quasi-uniform. The various factions fighting in Macedonia wore their own clothing with the addition of insignia or religious tokens which

Photographed in his natural setting, a typical pre-war Macedonian guerrilla leader poses in quasi-military clothing. He wears the traditional Macedonian cap, with a civilian jacket and trousers; high on his left sleeve is some kind of field sign, probably in the Greek national colours of white and blue. He is armed with a Gras M1874 carbine, and also has a handgun at his left hip.

LEFT **Most of these Ottoman soldiers in the mountains of Albania wear the M1909 uniform with the old-pattern red fez, but the bugler in the left background seems to have the old dark blue tunic. Interestingly, the Albanian irregular in the foreground, wearing a white skull cap and civilian clothing, has a certain air of authority about him. As a local pro-Ottoman Albanian leader he may have been given charge of this squad of regular soldiers.**

For warmth in the bitter winter, half of these Montenegrin soldiers bringing in a walking-wounded comrade have acquired sheepskin surcoats to wear over their M1910 uniforms. They are all armed with the Russian 7.62mm Mosin-Nagant M1891 rifle, introduced into Montenegrin service in 1898.

served as 'field signs' (Plate H2). Most Albanians fought in their traditional clothing (Plate H3), although some pro-Turkish volunteers were issued with dark blue Ottoman Army tunics dating from the 1890s. Ottoman irregulars such as the *Bashi-basouks* wore civilian clothing, with the odd military item issued when available.

Winter clothing

The campaigns of the Balkan Wars were often fought in rugged terrain and terrible conditions, and the winter of 1912–13 was a particularly severe one. Greatcoats were the standard winter wear for the more fortunate soldiers, but shortages meant that obsolete military and civilian coats were also worn.

The **Ottoman Army** had a modern double-breasted greatcoat made from grey wool, with a large collar that tightened snugly around the neck by means of a cord, and a fitted hood for extra protection. Many soldiers also went to war with the old pre-1908 dark blue double-breasted coat, which was piped in the branch colour. Officers had a grey-green double-breasted coat with a branch-coloured collar to go with their M1909 uniform, or could alternatively wear a hooded woollen 'mantle' or cloak.

Following the Russian style, the **Bulgarian Army** had a standard greatcoat in grey wool, double-breasted but with purely decorative buttons down the centre, and soldiers were also issued with a separate item of winter clothing, called in Bulgarian a *bashlak*. This was a long woollen scarf with a hood at one end; when the hood was being worn the rest of the *bashlak* was wrapped around the neck for extra warmth. Winter fleece or fur hats were also worn by the Bulgarians; these came in various sizes, with some artillerymen wearing a tall pointed version based on traditional peasant types. The 1890-issue black lambswool hat was worn when available during the winter of 1912–13, along with various locally made sheepskin hats.

Greek Army soldiers wore a single-breasted greatcoat in the same khaki wool as the rest of the uniform. Their officers had a short double-breasted winter coat, but might wear raincoats – like officers of all armies, they purchased their own clothing.

Serbian I Ban soldiers also wore a double-breasted coat in the same colour as the uniform, while II Ban men wore old dark blue models from the 1890s or even earlier. Dark blue greatcoats were still in widespread use by the Serbians in 1914, since Serbia had no time to replenish its uniform stocks from the 1912–13 fighting before the outbreak of the Great War.

In the **Montenegrin Army** officially prescribed winter gear was mainly confined to the officers, although an enlisted-ranks' greatcoat was specified in the 1910 dress regulations. Higher-ranking officers had a double-breasted greatcoat while more junior ranks had a hooded cloak. The ordinary Montenegrin soldiers often wore civilian coats, and many used sheepskin cloaks in the severe winter conditions.

PLATE COMMENTARIES

Shortages of uniforms, weapons and equipment

All nations taking part in the Balkan Wars were largely unprepared for the scale of the conflict. They all relied heavily on their mobilized reserve troops, and these soldiers often had to be supplied with any uniforms that happened to be available. To complicate matters, most of these armies were in the process of introducing modern khaki or grey-green uniforms; these new, practical field uniforms were usually available to the small regular armies, but there were not enough in store for the much larger numbers of reservists who were mobilized. Consequently, reserve troops often had to make do with older 19th-century coloured uniforms. (For example, the Serbian Army even used some obsolete Ottoman stocks that it had captured in the war of 1876–77.)

As the newer drab field uniforms wore out in use, soldiers of all the combatant nations often wore items from their dress uniforms, and this mixture of new and old garments produced a rag-tag appearance that epitomized the Balkan Wars, straddling the old and new styles of military clothing. As the war went on most countries placed orders abroad for new uniforms, equipment and weapons, but few of these were delivered before the end of the conflict. Captured uniform stocks were pressed into service by the soldiers in the field to make up for shortages. Again, during the war large stores of Ottoman uniforms were captured in supply depots by the Bulgarians and Serbs, and some of these were issued to needy units (presumably with any Turkish insignia removed first).

A: OTTOMAN ARMY

A1: *Nizam* regular infantryman, 1912

This Ottoman regular army soldier is wearing the M1909 uniform made of brown-khaki wool. In 1912 some Ottoman soldiers wore this khaki-coloured soft hat instead of the old pre-1909 red fez, but it was not in service for long, and was soon to be replaced with the familiar *enver* hat of 1914–18. Privates in the infantry had no tunic shoulder straps or collar patches. This soldier is in full marching order, with a knapsack and haversack in addition to his brown leather belt with ammunition pouches. The star-and-crescent device on his belt buckle was a common feature on most Ottoman uniforms of the period. His rifle is the 7.65mm Mauser M1903, the most modern of several Mauser models then in service with the Ottoman Army.

A2: *Rediff* reservist infantryman, Kırmastı Regiment; Chataldzha Line, 1912

This local reservist infantryman is part of the defence force manning the Chataldzha defensive lines on the road to Constantinople. As a *rediff* soldier he has been issued with an old and well-worn M1893 dark blue tunic, with the red trim of the infantry. He wears the old-pattern red felt fez with blue tassel, which had been emblematic of the Ottoman soldier for generations. The 1893 pattern trousers have red piping down the outseam, and are worn with wrapped woollen leggings secured by leather straps. Shoes were in short supply; this reservist has acquired a pair of comfortable locally-made peasant shoes. His regulation equipment is the leather belt and pouches, but he has also been issued with a bandolier carrying extra ammunition for his Mauser M1890 – a model still in widespread service in 1912.

trooper's equipment is basic: a belt supporting an enlisted-ranks' sabre and a single ammunition pouch. His carbine is the standard cavalry-issue 7.65mm Mauser M1905.

B: OTTOMAN ARMY

B1: Sergeant of Gendarmerie, 1912

This Ottoman military policeman is wearing a *kalpak* with the red top of the Gendarmerie. Even a member of an elite corps like this has had to be issued with the old-pattern blue tunic while he waits for a complete M1909 issue; it is trimmed with his red branch colour, and his rank is shown by the cloth sleeve chevrons. The yellow aiguillette and brass gorget are distinguishing signs of the gendarmes; the latter is inscribed *Kanun Neferi* – 'law soldier'. All his other uniform items are newly issued M1909 pattern, but shortages are indicated by his Peabody-Martini M1874 rifle, which should have been withdrawn from service by 1912.

B2: Captain of Engineers, 1913

By the outbreak of the fighting in 1912 most front-line Ottoman officers were wearing their new M1909 grey-green service dress. This captain of Engineers has the standard officers' uniform, with the tunic collar in the blue of that branch of service. On the blue cloth shoulder boards his rank is displayed by the two silver stars of captain on a gold braid base. The branch colour is repeated on the top surface of his astrakhan wool *kalpak* hat, with gold braiding in a crisscross pattern running from the edge into the centre to form a six-pointed star shape. Officers would usually purchase uniform items themselves; this captain has bought a pair of leather gaiters to go with his officers' boots, and a pair of gloves. He has armed himself with a Mauser C96 'broomhandle' semi-automatic pistol with a wooden holster-stock – an expensive weapon for any but the wealthiest of officers.

B3: Lieutenant-General, 1912

Senior Ottoman officers usually wore the light grey lambswool *kalpak*, with in this case a red top for the infantry branch. He wears a more expensively tailored example of the M1909 service dress; in 1912 infantry officers did not have branch-coloured collars, but red collar-piping. The general's rank is indicated on his 'Austrian knot'-pattern gold shoulder boards with a single star in the centre. His tailored woollen breeches have two red stripes down the outseam, and are tucked into officers' high boots. Although most officers would probably have had a pistol of some kind, this general is armed only with his officers' sabre.

C: BULGARIAN ARMY

C1 : Captain, 10th Infantry Regiment, 1912

This company commander wears the Bulgarian officers' standard field uniform in green-khaki cloth, with peaked cap, tunic and breeches. His cap has the red band of the infantry branch, bearing the national cockade in enamelled metal. The tunic has concealed buttons down the front, and is piped on the collar and cuffs in infantry red. On his shoulder boards his rank is shown by three silver stars on a gold braid background with a red central line, and his unit by the silver Roman numerals '10'. He has red trim down the

Mahmud Shevket Pasha (1858–1913), a general pictured wearing the officers' M1909 khaki tunic with the old-fashioned red fez; compare with Plate B3. This prominent Ottoman commander was a supporter of the 'Young Turks' movement, and played an important role in the overthrow of Sultan Abdul Hamid in 1909. He commanded operations against Malissori rebels in 1910–11, and fought in Albania again in 1912. He was appointed minister of war in summer 1912, but was assassinated by his political enemies in June 1913.

A3: Trooper of regular cavalry; Adrianople, 1913

This Ottoman regular cavalryman is part of a detachment which rode into Adrianople during the Second Balkan War under the command of Maj Mustafa Kemal (better known by his title of Attaturk, adopted when he became the founder and leader of the modern Turkish state in the 1920s). The trooper is wearing the M1909 khaki uniform with cavalry boots, and a headgear first seen during the 1912–13 campaign. This *kabalak* was described as being improvised with strips of woollen cloth wound around a wicker frame. From photographic evidence it appears that it was often quite poorly constructed and presented an untidy appearance, with strips of cloth hanging loosely down. The

outseam of his breeches, and his officers' high boots have spurs attached. His weapons are an officers' sabre and a P08 Parabellum (Luger) semi-automatic pistol, and he has also purchased a pair of binoculars from an officers' outfitters in Sofia before leaving for the front.

C2: Second lieutenant, 2nd Artillery Regiment, 1913
This figure illustrates the improvisation that was often unavoidable because of uniform shortages during the wars. His peaked cap has the black branch-colour band of the artillery, displaying the usual enamelled cockade. Because his green-khaki field tunic has worn out he has had to resort to wearing that of his pre-1906 dark blue dress uniform. His leg- and footwear is regulation. The belt, also from his dress uniform, carries the holster for his Mannlicher M1905 semi-automatic pistol.

C3: Volunteer, Macedonian-Adrianopolitan Volunteer Corps, 1912
Volunteers for the pro-Bulgarian MAVC were officially issued with uniforms, but, like many of his comrades, this man is wearing his own paramilitary dress. The brass badge of the MAVC is displayed on his lambswool hat. His greenish khaki-coloured quasi-military jacket is privately purchased, as are his trousers. He has given himself a more military appearance by wearing brown woollen puttees, but has only *tsarvuli* peasant shoes. His equipment is basic: a leather waist bandolier with large clip pouches, and a bandolier over his shoulder. He is fortunate to have been issued with a modern Bulgarian Army Mannlicher M1890 carbine.

D: BULGARIAN ARMY

D1 : Private, 22nd Infantry Regiment (His Royal Highness Prince Edward of Saxe-Coburg's)
The elite 'patron regiments' would have attracted the best recruits, and had distinctive uniform facings and insignia. This private of the 22nd Infantry has white cap trim instead of the standard red, a gold-edged collar, and a gold-painted 'ESK' monogram on his shoulder straps. The leather marching boots seem to have been characteristic of the 'patron regiments'. His equipment is standard issue, the leather belt supporting two pouches, his bayonet scabbard and a metal canteen. The rifle in this case is the 8mm M1895, the most modern of several Mannlicher models then in Bulgarian service.

D2: Volunteer, *Narodno Opolcenie*, 1913
This middle-aged reservist who has come forward to serve in the territorial militia wears mainly civilian clothing. One item of uniform is his fleece hat, displaying a brass badge of the Bulgarian royal coat of arms. His jacket, waistcoat and shirt are his own; his uniform trousers may have been issued, or given to him by a relative in the military. Around his lower legs are wrapped *navushta* leggings held in place with gartering that was originally made from horsehair, but in this case of wool; like C3, he has not been issued with boots so has to wear his *tsarvuli* shoes. Equipment is limited to a single ammunition pouch, and a blanket roll that contains his personal belongings. He carries the bayonet fixed on his Russian-donated Berdan rifle.

Mixed group of Ottoman troops in Albania, 1912. The man on the left is identifed as a gendarme or military policeman by the brass gorget and yellow aiguillettes – see Plate B1, although all these men appear to have khaki uniforms, with fezzes in red or khaki, or astrakhan hats.

D3: Private, 5th Infantry Regiment
This illustrates the standard 'tobacco-brown' uniform worn by most Bulgarian infantrymen in 1912. The peaked cap has a blue top and is piped in red, with a frontal tricolour cockade in the Bulgarian national colours (white-green-red, reading inwards). His tunic bears no rank insignia, but the regimental number is marked in gold paint on the shoulder straps. Because of a shortage of military boots the matching trousers are worn with peasant footwear – white cloth leggings (*navushta*), held in place by woollen tapes (*vurvi*), and shoes (*tsarvuli*) that are rather too light to withstand prolonged marching. In addition to the belt with pouches holding the five-round clips for his 8mm Mannlicher M1880/90 rifle, he has full marching equipment including a knapsack, a tent section with wooden poles, and a water canteen.

E: ROMANIAN & MONTENEGRIN ARMIES

E1: Private, Romanian 7th Reserve Infantry Regiment, 1913
The Romanian troops that invaded Bulgaria in 1913 wore a wide variety of uniforms including the old M1893 blue, the new M1912 grey-green, or mixtures of items from both; this reservist has a complete M1893 uniform. The leather-peaked dark blue field cap which was introduced in that year, and the dark blue tunic, are piped in infantry red; both the cap and the shoulder straps bear the red regimental number. The grey woollen trousers are piped red down the outseam, and tucked into high marching boots. He wears full marching equipment with knapsack and tent section. Note that the Romanian 6.5mm Mannlicher M1893 rifle was issued to all tiers of the army in 1913.

E2: Corporal, Romanian 16th Infantry Regiment, 1913

This is the newly-issued M1912 grey-green woollen uniform piped in infantry red, with spearhead-shaped collar patches of the same colour. Versions of this distinctive *capela* field cap were worn by the Romanian Royal Army from 1893 until 1945. Note the regimental number stitched both on the front of this cloth-peaked version of the cap, and on his red-piped shoulder straps, which also show his two yellow rank bars. In addition to his M1891 black leather equipment he has a canvas haversack with an integral pocket for his canteen. His rifle is the standard-issue 6.5mm Mannlicher M1893, which was used alongside smaller numbers of the M1892 model.

E3: Montenegrin standard-bearer, 9th Durmitorska Brigade, 1912

Most of the soldiers of the Montenegrin Army of 1912 were dressed like this, in traditional regional dress which served as a uniform. On his *kapitza* cap he has the brass oval badge, with the Montenegrin crown over the Cyrillic cypher of King Nicholas – 'H1' – bordered with a wreath. His costume otherwise comprises a *doloma* jacket, *jalek* waistcoat and *shalwar* trousers. Tucked into his *rushak* sash is an example of the widely-used Gasser revolver, in this case an M1870/74 Montenegrin model. The design of the battalion standard dates from 1871; it bears the royal coat of arms with the king's cypher in the centre.

E4: Corporal, Montenegrin infantry, 1912

This soldier taking part in the assault on Ottoman-held Scutari wears the new M1910 uniform, with its pillbox cap for enlisted ranks; this version of the brass cap badge was particular to his rank. Officers' uniforms under the 1910 regulations were similar, but the younger and more modern-minded officers wore a peaked cap instead. His equipment is limited to a Russian-supplied M1893 belt with ammunition pouches, and a blanket roll. His M1891 Mosin-Nagant rifle is one of 20,000 supplied by Russia in 1898–99 to replace the old Berdan rifle, which was then passed on to second-line troops.

F: SERBIAN ARMY

F1: Private, 6th Infantry Regiment, Drina Division, 1912

This private of the Serbian 'First Ban' or regular army is wearing the M1908 khaki woollen uniform with the *sajcaka* frontier cap. The way that the *sajcaka* was worn varied greatly from soldier to soldier; some lifted the crown up and others wore it pushed down. His single-breasted tunic has the red collar patches of the infantry, and his regimental number is displayed in gold Roman numerals on his shoulder straps; note the roll at the end of his right strap, to retain his rifle sling. The trousers are tucked into thick woollen peasant socks, which are worn with traditional *opanci* shoes. He has two cartridge pouches, a blanket roll and a metal canteen. Most first-line troops were issued this 7mm Mauser M1910 rifle.

F2: Infantryman, II Ban, 1912

Second-line (II Ban) soldiers were often dressed in the old M1896 double-breasted tunic or *kaporan*. This has the red collar, shoulder straps and piping of the infantry, and fastens

Bulgarian officers of an unidentified unit in 1912, wearing the officers' grey greatcoat with blue collar, and collar patches and hat band in their branch colour – the tone suggests black, for either Artillery or Engineers. Unfortunately both the regimental number and the ranks on the shoulder boards are unclear here, although both men are probably lieutenants. Note the striped cloth waist belts, and gold dress pouch belts over the left shoulder. Both officers have sabres, and on their right hips holstered pistols with neck lanyards.

down the right with concealed studs or buttons. Both his *sajcaka* frontier cap and trousers are made from a dark grey wool material, and the latter are tucked into an old pair of low leather marching boots from the 1890s. His equipment is also 19th century, and includes a hide-covered knapsack. Second Ban soldiers were given whatever rifles were available, in this case a Russian-made M1887 Berdan.

F3: Captain, 4th Heavy Artillery Battery, Third Army, 1913

Serbian officers wore the M1908 uniform with either a peaked or a peakless cap which was based on the *sajcaka*; this captain has the peakless version, displaying the officers' enamelled cockade in white-blue-red (reading inwards). His tunic collar is in the black branch-colour of the artillery, and

Although originally captioned 'Serbian reservists read news of war', this photograph shows clothing typically worn by both Serbian and Bulgarian reserve troops – compare with Plate D2. Many of the second-line troops of the Balkan League armies would have been veterans of late 19th-century campaigns. The Serbian veterans might have fought against the Bulgarians in the Serbian-Bulgarian war of 1885; and older Bulgarians might have fought in the Bulgarian Legion in the Russo-Turkish War of 1877–78.

note also the black cuff piping. The shoulder boards have black edging and central stripe, gold braid inner edging, a Roman battery number, and the three silver four-pointed stars of his rank. His breeches are worn with black leather gaiters and low boots. A leather valise or holdall case hangs on his left hip from a belt worn beneath his tunic, and the holster for his Russian Nagant M1895 revolver is slung on a strap over his left shoulder.

F4: Volunteer, III Ban, 1912
The Serbian 'Third Ban' was a civilian militia that received little if any uniform or equipment, and volunteers had to provide their own clothing. In this case a lambswool *subara* hat is worn with a double-breasted reefer-style jacket, cotton shirt, loose-fitting peasant trousers, leggings secured with strips of cloth, and *opanci* shoes. The only equipment he has is the canvas haversack, which he may have brought from home. He probably carries in his pockets the ammunition for his Mauser M1871 rifle; the Russian-made Berdan II of the same vintage was also used by the III Ban in 1912–13.

G: GREEK ARMY

G1: Sergeant, 7th Evzones Battalion, 1912
This elite light infantry branch earned a formidable fighting reputation, and wore a distinctive uniform. The olive-khaki *farizan* cap, badged with the gold-crowned national cockade in blue-white-blue, had a long black tassel attached to the top when out of the line, but this was removed before going into combat. The traditional folk costume of these highlanders consisted of a tight-fitting shirt and a multi-pleated kilt or *foustenella*, its 40 pleats symbolizing the 400 years of

Romanian artilleryman wearing the lightweight summer version of the grey-green M1912 uniform and cap; his branch is identified by the black collar patches, and black piping and crossed-cannons badge on the cap. This light infantry blouse, seen worn by some Romanian troops in 1913, was formally introduced into service in 1916. His trousers seem to be of an old dark blue pattern from the 1890s. His carbine is the Austrian Mannlicher M1893, issued to both the Romanian cavalry and artillery. (Courtesy Ablibris)

Although this Greek soldier appears to be an infantryman wearing the standard M1908 uniform, magnification suggests that he could be an artilleryman. His buttons show a crossed-cannons and shell device, which means that his shoulder straps should be madder-red. His puttees are non-regulation, but were more practical than letting the straight-leg trousers hang loose. The M1895 brown leather equipment has ammunition pouches for his Mannlicher-Schönauer M1903 rifle (see Plate G3); note how this is displayed for the camera, with the bolt open and a five-round clip in the lips of the magazine.

Ottoman rule. This long, deep-collared *doulama* jacket – red-piped at collar and cuff, and with infantry-red shoulder straps – was a more practical alternative. The sergeant's rank is indicated by the two red-backed gold stripes on the lower sleeves. Thick off-white woollen hose were worn, with the black tassels which hung from the garters below the knees removed before battle, when some Evzones also seem to have covered their hose with khaki over-trousers. Again, the large black pompons traditionally worn on the *tsarouchia*

shoes were removed before battle; made from red-dyed pigskin, these shoes were heavily hob-nailed. This NCO carries the standard-issue Mannlicher-Schönauer M1903 rifle, and has minimal leather equipment.

G2: Captain of Engineers, 1913
The Greek Army officers' uniform consisted of an olive-khaki cap, tunic and breeches. The képi-style cap has a brown

leather peak and chinstrap, and piping in the engineers' blue branch colour round the top of the band and up the quarters of the crown. It displays the crowned national cockade, and metallic braid stripes around the band (gold for infantry, silver for cavalry and engineers). The tunic is piped in blue on the stand collar, front edge and cuffs, and has blue shoulder boards with the three silver stars of his rank set on a gold braid central stripe. The olive-khaki breeches, also piped with engineer-blue, are worn with high brown-leather field boots with gaiter-style legs. His brown leather belt carries the holster for his French M1892 revolver.

G3: Private, 4th Infantry Regiment, 1912

The M1908 olive-khaki woollen uniform is worn with an M1910 cap piped in the red of the infantry, with a brown leather peak and chinstrap, and the crowned cockade on the front. The tunic has infantry-red piping on the collar and cuffs, and red shoulder straps bearing the regimental number in black stitching. The red-piped trousers are worn here loose over his brown boots; this was found to be impractical, and puttees were soon adopted. The M1895 brown leather equipment is worn, with a knapsack and canvas haversack. The three belt pouches hold 150 rounds for his Austrian-made Mannlicher-Schönauer M1903 rifle.

G4: Volunteer, Italian Legion, 1912

The Italians who came to fight for Greece in 1912 were fully armed and equipped by the Greek Army. They were issued with Greek Army caps and tunics which had been dyed red as a compliment to these Garibaldini, so that they could maintain the famous tradition of their red-shirted forebears of the 1860s. This volunteer has buttoned a sun curtain in plain olive-khaki to his red cap. His red-piped olive-khaki trousers, khaki puttees, brown leather boots and equipment, and M1903 rifle are all standard Greek issue.

H: IRREGULAR VOLUNTEERS

H1: Greek volunteer guard, Zographou Monastery, Mount Athos, 1913

This local volunteer is part of the 'Sacred Company' which successfully defeated the Bulgarian troops guarding Zographou Monastery on Mt Athos in southern Macedonia in June 1913. The semi-official Greek garrisons for the many monasteries on the 'holy mountain' were made up of a mixture of gendarmes, home guardsmen, and even unordained monks; some irregular volunteers also travelled from far away to defend these shrines of the Greek Orthodox faith. Although wearing little in the way of regular uniform or equipment items, this irregular has a Greek Army cap badge, and shows his allegiance by an armband and the cross hanging from his neck. Typically, he is armed with old Greek Army weapons – a Gras M1874 rifle, and a St Etienne M1874 revolver tucked into one of his bandit-style cartridge belts.

H2: Volunteer, *Makedonimachoi*, Macedonia, 1912

Among the very diverse population of Macedonia, many followers of the Greek Orthodox faith fought for the Greek Army. Numbers of these 'Macedonian fighters' had previously fought against the Ottoman Army during a major rebellion against Turkish rule in 1903. This volunteer is wearing civilian clothing adapted for military service, and

Two proud-looking Albanian guerrillas pose for a studio photograph. Although their traditional costume resembles that in Plate H3, the white caps show that they are Muslims, serving the Ottoman Army as scouts or irregulars. They are armed with short Peabody-Martini M1874 short rifles, and have Gasser revolvers tucked into their waist bandoliers.

brown leather equipment. He has attached a chevron arrangement of blue and white ribbons at his left shoulder as a Greek field sign, to distinguish him from his Bulgarian enemies fighting in the IMRO. Note, again, the silver pectoral cross which he displays as a further sign of his allegiance to the Patriarch. Although most *Makedonimachoi* were armed with Gras M1874 rifles, this man has acquired an ex-Ottoman Winchester 1866; his holstered revolver is an old 1873 Beaumont Adams.

H3: *Malisorri* volunteer, Montenegrin Army, 1912

In the highly confused situation in Albania in 1912–13, local populations also found themselves embroiled in the fighting. The *Malisorri* people of northern Albania were adherents of the Roman Catholic church, and some of them volunteered to fight for the understrength Montenegrin Army. Issued with obsolete Montenegrin or captured Turkish rifles and employed as auxiliary fighters, the *Malisorri* wore traditional Albanian dress, but were usually pictured wearing white headscarves instead of the Muslim white skull cap. This volunteer has been given an Austrian Werndl M1873 rifle, as used by the Montenegrin Army in the late 19th century, and has also acquired a Montenegrin-issue Gasser revolver.

INDEX

References to illustrations are shown in **bold**. Plates are in **bold**, with captions on the page in brackets.